# Pat Moran

## (1961-1992) A RETROSPECTIVE

GANDON EDITIONS

PAT MORAN (1961-1992) – A RETROSPECTIVE

Published to coincide with the Pat Moran retrospective exhibition at the Crawford Municipal Art Gallery, Cork, and the Dunamaise Arts Centre Portlaoise.

Editors          Claire Carpenter, Hugh Lorigan,
                 Anthony Lyttle, Dorothy Smith,
                 Bridget Webster

© Compilation copyright Gandon Editions and the Pat Moran Retrospective, 2003. All rights reserved.

ISBN             0948037 016

Design           John O'Regan (© Gandon, 2002)
Production        Nicola Dearey, Gandon
Photography       Sam Gallagher, Nigel Swann
Printing          Nicholson & Bass, Belfast
Distribution      Gandon Distribution, Kinsale

GANDON EDITIONS
Oysterhaven, Kinsale, Co Cork, Ireland

tel / fax        +353 (0)21-4770830 / 4770755
e-mail           gandon@eircom.net
web-site         www.gandon-editions.com

Gandon Editions is grant-aided by The Arts Council

CRAWFORD MUNICIPAL ART GALLERY
Emmet Place, Cork, Ireland

tel / fax        +353 (0)21-4273377 / 4805043
e-mail           crawfordgallery@eircom.net
web-site         www.crawfordartgallery.com

exhibition       28 February – 5 April 2003

DUNAMAISE ARTS CENTRE
Portlaoise, Co Laois

tel / fax        +353 (0)502-63355
e-mail           dunamaise@eircom.net
web-site         www.dunamaisetheatre.com

exhibition       11 April – 1 May 2003

EXHIBITION CREDITS

Transportation   Tony Magennis,
                 Fine Art Transport and Installation
Insurances       PJT Insurance Services
Web Design       Equinox e-Business Solutions
Production        Claire Carpenter, Hugh Lorigan,
                 Anthony Lyttle, Dorothy Smith,
                 Bridget Webster

For additional information, visit: www.patmoran.org

All material collected in relation to this publication and exhibition is held at the National Irish Visual Arts Library, National College of Art & Design, 100 Thomas Street, Dublin 8

This publication was part-financed by the Crawford Municipal Art Gallery, Cork

ILLUSTRATIONS

cover            Gardiner Street, 1984, oil on canvas,
                 147 x 99 cm
pre-title        Bird, 1992, ink on paper
frontispiece     Self-Portrait, 1983, watercolour,
                 16 x 12 cm

* The bird and flower come from an enamel badge found pinned to the mantlepiece in Pat's studio. Cast in bronze, it was set in stone by Studio 16 on the shore of the lake where Pat lost his life on Sherkin Island in 1992.

# Contents

*Italian Landscape*
1984, mixed media on paper,
21 x 30 cm

# Tribute

RICHARD GORMAN

P at Moran painted pictures, and he painted pictures of what he knew and experienced. Vertigo from a window looking down onto Gardiner Street and warped traffic. The honesty to paint cars – no one paints cars in the romance language of cityscape. Giddily leaning lampposts clawing in to blue and green streetscapes. Black and white expressions of inner-city grubbiness.

Pat painted as he lived, with vitality and directness, and of course in the usual confusions of our being. Paintings based in knowledge of art history – Pat had a classical leaning, a Roman aspect, even physically.

RICHARD GORMAN is an artist.

Pat Moran photographed at Dun Laoghaire School of Art, 1982

# Foreword

This retrospective exhibition and publication celebrate the life and work of an artist and a friend – a man who best summed up his philosophy of life with the following oft-repeated quote from *The Tailor and Ansty* by Eric Cross: "The world is only a blue bag, knock a squeeze out of it when you can."

— Claire Carpenter, Hugh Lorigan, Anthony Lyttle,
Dorothy Smith, Bridget Webster

ACKNOWLEDGEMENTS

*Supporters of the project:*
Dimitri Broë, Campbell Bruce, Julian Campbell, Stella Coffey, Cork Artists Collective, Charlie Cullen, Paul Darcy, Aidan Dunne, Nuala Fenton, Sandy Fitzgerald, Jack Gilligan, Richard Gorman, Paddy Graham, Brian Maguire, Peter Murray, Rory O'Byrne, Mick O'Dea, Gwen O'Dowd, Vera Ryan, Una Sealy, John Taylor, Pat Taylor

*Very special thanks to artists who contributed pieces of work to the sale to fund this book and retrospective:*
Pauline Bewick, Mary Canty, Claire Carpenter, Comghall Casey, Felicity Clear, Eamon Colman, Eamon Connors, Margaret Corcoran, Jim Cummins, Barbara Dunne, Andrew Folan, Billy Foley, Mary Avril Gillan, Richard Gorman, Sheila Gorman, Wendy Judge, Orla Kaminska, Paul Laroque, Mo Levy, Róisín Lewis, Hugh Lorigan, Anthony Lyttle, Leo McCann, Dave McCormack, Tom McGuirk, Ruth McHugh, Louise Meade, Nick Miller, Philip Moss, Niall Neassans, Collette Nolan, Kathleen O'Brien, Meadbh O'Byrne, Mick O'Dea, Gwen O'Dowd, Juan Perez, Connor Regan, Mark Reilly, James Scanlon, Una Sealy, Dorothy Smith, Margaret Tuffy

*Donations in support of the book and retrospective:*
Bruce Arnold, Ann and Sidney Carpenter, Jeremy Carpenter, Susan Donovan, Gerry Kilby, Deirbhle McCann-Henry, Breeda Mooney, Max and Anne Wilson, Ruairí Ó Siocháin

*All the people who lent their paintings for this publication and the exhibition:*
Paul Moloney of AXA Ireland, Clodagh and Hillard Bryan, Anne and Sydney Carpenter, Claire Carpenter, Jeremy Carpenter and Susan Donovan, Justine Carpenter and John Cole, Austin Carroll, Brian Connolly, Crawford Municipal Art Gallery, Jeremy Eng, Darragh Feely, Declan Feely, Kay and Kevin Feely, Willy Finnye and Jenny Adamson, Patrick Gageby, Annette Henessey, Charlie Henessey, Jim and Maíre Hughes, Tim and Sarah Hughes, Niamh and Banbha Henry, Eleanor Howard, Gerry Kilby, Eva and Ian Kitchen, Dr and Mrs Lorigan, Hugh Lorigan, Paul Lorigan, Deirbhle McCann-Henry, Robert Maharry, Brian Moran, J&M Moran, Niamh Moran, Tom and Anne Moran, John Norris, Jacquie Moore of the Office of Public Works, Sunniva O'Flynn, Ruairí Ó Siocháin, Dave and Elma O'Sullivan, Portlaoise Prison, John Ryan, Shiela Pratchke of Tyrone Guthrie Centre, Bridget Webster

*Special thanks to:*
Richard Callanan, Cois Céim Dance Theatre, Aidan Dunne, Feely family, Richard Gorman, Mark Kavanagh, Gerry Kilby, Tom McGuirk, John Meany, Miriam Kehoe, Patricia Lawlor and Louise Donlon at Dunamaise Arts Centre, Peter Murray and Dawn Williams at the Crawford Gallery, Moran family, Studio 16 artists, Nigel Swann, Temple Bar Properties

*Gasometer, Ringsend*   1992, pencil on paper, 21 x 29 cm      *Leeson Street*   1990, pencil on paper, 24 x 33 cm

*Leeson Street*   1990, pencil on paper, 24 x 33 cm         *Amiens Street*    1992, pencil on paper, 12 x 18 cm

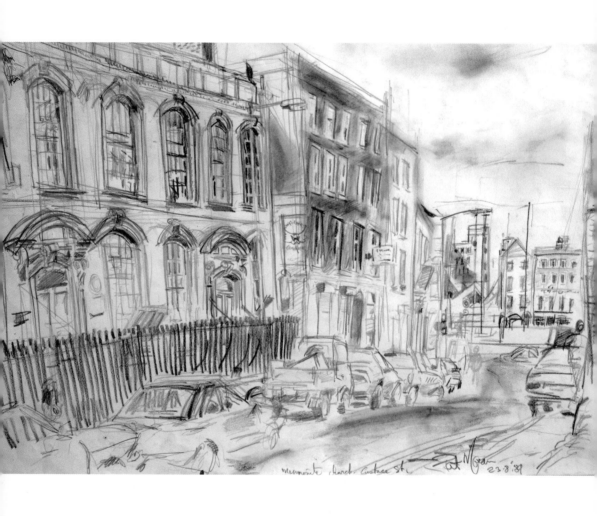

*Eustace Street*
1989, pencil on paper, 42 x 60 cm

# Pat Moran

AIDAN DUNNE

Writing about Barrie Cooke ten years ago, the Dutch curator Rudi Fuchs aligned him with an alternative tradition of European artistic outsiders. He meant outsider not in the sense of what used to be termed primitive or unschooled, but outside the classical, modern tradition of 20th-century painting which, Fuchs suggested, took its cue from Cézanne's analytical eye. Some artists proved unamenable to the regularising, utopian vision of formalism and abstraction, and were instinctively drawn to the messy irregularity of the world. Cooke, Fuchs said, was one of those; so too were Jack B Yeats, Oscar Kokoschka, Chaim Soutine, Georges Rouault, Per Kirkeby and several more. It should be immediately obvious, by the way the mere mention of several of these names strikes a chord in relation to Pat Moran's work, that he too would be quite at home in Fuchs' band of outsiders.

It is true that the differences between Cooke and Pat Moran are more obvious than their similarities. Where the former is drawn to nature, to wild rural environments, the latter is, in his work, comfortably at home in the city. Nonetheless, there is common ground. What they have in common is a commitment to capturing the living pulse of the subject. It is the sense of real-time engagement with something vital and unpredictable that gives Pat Moran's work its exceptional, excited liveliness. This is at the heart of what Fuchs identifies as a distinct tradition. Unruly reality – contingent and volatile, beyond the artist's direct control – is interesting in a way that orderly predictability can never be.

There is a popular view of Yeats as a painter of romanticised Irish landscape, but his landscapes invariably hinge on aspects of dramatic narratives, and his earlier work is notable for its immersion in communal life in Dublin and Sligo. Which brings us to Kokoschka. It's difficult to think of a painter who infused his subjects with more nervous energy than Oscar Kokoschka, though with Pat Moran's 1990 self-portrait – head turned, glowing cigarette clamped between his lips, one eyebrow arched inquisitorially, caught against his own work, bordered by painterly paraphernalia and, beyond, the world outside the window that fed his imagination – we surely come pretty close. And apart from portraits of people, Kokoschka pioneered what might be described as portraits of cities, something that is particularly relevant to Pat Moran.

Working in Dublin, particularly in Gardiner Street, and then in Cork, Moran was someone who was clearly much taken with the communal nature of city life. There was never a question of mere bricks and mortar. When he drew or painted a street, it is always distorted though the lens of momentary, chance, subjective observation, and it is alive with the beehive hum of busy habitation, the non-stop flow of pedestrian and mechanised traffic. This fascination with communal space and energy is integral to his way of seeing, so his involvement in several collaborative mural projects, and his interest in the Mexican muralists, were in no sense diversions or departures, they were a logical and consistent development of his central concerns as an artist. Given that everything he did was steeped in a sense of community, he had no distance to travel to community arts. He was, by instinct and inclination, a community artist to begin with.

In much of Moran's work there is the Kokoschka-like view of the city as a vast, sprawling, organism. Typically, even the streets, pavements, shopfronts and buildings have a respiratory flexibility. Clouds scud restlessly across the sky and every surface is animated by a dancing, variable sunlight. (He also liked the fluidity of electric light, the way it glows, spills and flows.) What might come across as being entirely haphazard and fragmented – the chaotic jumble of city life – is allowed a certain anarchic energy, but is also seen as coherent and homogeneous in a natural, self-regulating way. How so? Arguably, in the way that he favours a number of particular motifs that, although strictly isolated and fragmentary, can be viewed as representative of the city itself as a greater unity. There is the recurrent example of the street as a unit, and then such distinctive urban features as the hotel, railway station and cathedral. All can be regarded as symbolising larger scales and levels of urban organisation.

In his sinuous renditions, the modular nature of street or station, and their fundamental interconnectedness, direct us towards to the wider view. The cathedral – views of St Fin Barre's in Cork – is an embodiment of the exercise of huge communal skill and industry, with an intimation of transcendental purpose. Not a bad symbol for the city as a living thing, with its own incalculable character and personality, generated by the energy, aspirations and desires of the people who do not so much inhabit as comprise it.

Often the artist and we, the viewers, are in the position of being inside looking out on the city as spectacle, as, literally, street theatre. But the artist eavesdropping on the rush of the city from the vantage point of the studio highlights something that comes through again and again in Yeats. In the midst of communality, there is an anonymity to city life. There is an impersonality to the ceaseless flow of people and cars, all caught up in their own narratives, impelled by their own priorities, an impersonality that is only mitigated by the artist's role as narrator, and his integrative vision.

It is tragic that Pat Moran died just when he was preparing to return to Dublin. In some respects he may have sharpened his focus during his time in Cork, and he was poised to apply himself anew to what was already familiar territory. But it is more than clear from his existing work that he was completely in love with the messy irregularity of the world, that he harboured a cohesive vision of art and community, and that he possessed an unrivalled zest for life, a zest that is fully present in his painting.

AIDAN DUNNE is the art critic for *The Irish Times*, and has written extensively on Irish art.

*St Fin Barre's*   1990, pen and wash on paper, 60 x 42 cm

*I'm Dying for a Cig*
1984, pencil on paper, 33 x 24 cm

*Self Portrait*   1984, pencil on paper, 24 x 33 cm (detail)   *Self Portrait*   pencil on paper, 15 x 21 cm

*To Let*
pencil on paper, 38 x 56 cm

16

# Blue Notes

TOM McGUIRK

To describe oneself as having been a friend of the painter Pat Moran is by no means to claim to be part of an elite group. Among Pat's many talents was an extraordinary and inclusive gift for friendship. The sadness of his all-too-early death was magnified by the sheer numbers of those who grieved so openly. That a friend so sensitive to the colours of this world should have been so brutally plucked from them seemed then almost unbearable.

Defensively his friends consoled one another with thoughts of how fulsomely Pat had lived his foreshortened life. It is only now, perhaps, and particularly with this exhibition, that something of our loss in terms of Pat's work can be seen in any true perspective. This exhibition is important in giving us such a perspective and allowing us to assess the work en masse. It also sadly, but of course inevitably, gives us a tantalising sense of what might have been.

Figurative and representational as Pats work is, it was never universally well received in his lifetime. I remember Pat having a particularly hard time in college where his work was out of sync with then-favoured versions of late modernism, one strain of which leant towards a bombastic abstract expressionism, which, in hindsight, has not aged particularly well. Pat's answer to that rendition of My Way was the highway that took him to Italy and later Mexico, but ultimately back home to Dublin and Cork – two cities intensely portrayed in the work in this show.

Pat's work belongs to an earlier modernist tradition, the inheritor of Romanticism's belief in the primacy of the individual's perception. As such it also ran against the conceptualist current of its time. The artist Sol LeWitt wrote that conceptual art, in order to be 'more mentally interesting' to the viewer, should become 'emotionally dry' and should minimise the importance of the object's physicality and to be free from 'the dependence of the skill of the artist as a craftsman'.[1] Conceptualism also minimised the importance of perception in the art-making processes. This view was foreign to Pat's makeup; his art could never have been moulded to fit such dogmatic constraints. Conceptual art has been defined as 'art which gives priority to an idea presented by visual means that are secondary to the idea'.[2]

In Pat's work the visual means are always primary. The works displayed here do not begin with an idea, but with something or other from our material world – the street's detritus, a human form, a pair of yellow slippers. From these things the work is wrought so that it might become an idea in the mind of the viewer. If Pat's approach to art-making seems old fashioned it is because it is as old as art itself.

Schopenhauer's view of the art-making process, represents the antithesis of the conceptualist views outlined above. He believed that all true art must be grounded in perception. To perceive, to allow the things themselves to speak to us, to apprehend and grasp new relations between them, and then to precipitate all this into concepts, in order to possess it with certainty – this is what gives us new knowledge. But whereas almost everyone is capable of comparing concepts with concepts, to compare concepts with perceptions is a gift of the select few.[3] Indeed, he said that 'the concept, useful as it is in life, and serviceable, necessary and productive as it is in science, is always barren in art.'[4] Pat's cityscapes conform to this view of art. They shimmer and contort, sway and buzz to an entirely subjective rhythm which represents their author's individual perception, of a transient world, ever in flux. His own features are likewise presented in flux through a miasma of cigarette-smoke in his jaunty, mocking self-portrait. No doubt Billie Holiday's voice is filling the studio air.

The link with music (particularly jazz and blues) in Pat's work is not superficial. Music is of course the art form which most readily touches our emotions, and Pat could never and would never eschew emotion in his work. Rhythm is everywhere in the work, as is the subjectivism associated with improvisation. He's telling it like he sees it in the unrepeatable moment, no objective distance, no apologies, no explanations. There is little aspiration to idealism or classical harmony either, instead we are treated to a solo composed of slipping glimpses, a subjective artist's-eye view of the world and the material things therein, which appeals directly to our ability to recognise the particular emotional chord struck.

Colour too has, of course, its musical equivalence and emotional resonance. Pat's colour is indebted to the saturated high notes of the modernism of artists like Matisse. Blue is a signature colour, not only in those boisterous cerulean and cobalt skies, but in the self-portraits or the streetscapes which have a bluesy downbeat quality. This cord however is never heavy or oppressive. Lightness is integral to Pat's work; his is a floating world full of movement and light. Pat's images act like riffs echoing in the mind. It may be difficult for some time to walk down Dublin's Gardiner Street without the hubbub of Pat's wonderfully windy drawing rattling in your head.

'So what's the big idea in Pat's art?' you might ask, but you'd be missing the point. There is no separation of the idea and the work itself. Of course there is a conceptual framework which emerges from the tradition of western figurative painting; however, the work begins with the concrete world and Pat's perception and response to it. Conceptualist approaches to art-making privilege idea and content over form and the materiality of the artwork. They attempt to impose a set of linguistic rules on the process of art-making in an appeal to the intellect over the emotions and the senses. In that way they are dualistic. Work like Pat's, in its spontaneity, rejects such strategies, refusing to be hidebound by artificial rules.

Pat's art, like much of creative activity, was grounded in his practice, and he evolved a practice which facilitated his instinct for spontaneity and improvisation. Jazz improvisation takes place more rapidly than the slower mental progress of language and conceptual thought. As when riding a bike, conceptual thought may even get in the way – too much thought about the mechanics of what you are doing will increase the likelihood of your falling off. As one commentator put it: 'Thinking about what you are doing degrades your ability to do it.'[5] Speaking about bicycle-riding, among other human skills, Michael Polanyi has said: 'Rules of art can be useful but they do not determine the practice of an art; they are maxims, which can serve as a guide to an art only if they can integrated into the practical knowledge of the art. They cannot replace that knowledge.'[6] Does that mean such art is somehow non-intellectual? Well only if you subscribe to a narrow, peculiarly western bias which dismisses the epistemological significance of purposeful action.

The artist's death has a strange effect on how we interpret the artwork. We are reminded that this is not a work in progress, this is the definitive version. Our view of the work changes. It becomes something fixed. This exhibition I believe will help us to fix Pat's work, if such a thing is possible in the case of such a vital and ebullient oeuvre. Separating the work and the life is not easy in Pat's case. The work is like the man – spontaneous, effervescent, emotionally available and life-affirming. This exhibition fittingly conjoins two of Pat's greatest talents – his artistic gifts represented here in the work itself, and an extraordinary gift for friendship. This is a show which could not have taken place without the selflessness of the organisers and his many other friends.

Life, as Pat was fond of saying, is a blue bag; the trick was to get a few squeezes out if it while you can. He managed to squeeze out more than most, and some of his efforts are visible to us here.

TOM McGUIRK is an artist and lecturer.

ENDNOTES

[1]  S Le Witt, 'Paragraphs on Conceptual Art', Artforum, 5, no.10 (June 1967) 79
[2]  E Langmuir and N Lynton (eds), The Yale Dictionary of Art and Artists (Yale University Press, New Haven and London) 154
[3]  Arthur Schopenhauer from The World as Will and Idea (1819), quoted in B Magee, Confessions of a Philosopher (Phoenix, London, 1998) 475
[4]  Schopenhauer, The World as Will and Idea, D Berman (ed.) (Everyman, London, 1995) 148
[5]  RE Cytowic, The Man Who Tasted Shapes (Abacus, London, 1994) 177
[6]  M Polanyi, Personal Knowledge: Towards a Post-Critical Philosophy (University of Chicago Press, 1974) 50

*Wumps and Claire*
1983, pencil and coloured pen on paper, 42 x 60 cm

*Flags on Liffey*
1988, pencil on paper, 24 x 33 cm

*Gardiner Street*
1984, charcoal, 76 x 50 cm

*Grow with Irish Life*
1985, mixed media on paper, 100 x 139 cm

*Night Bus*
1983, oil on board, 63 x 75 cm

*Gardiner Street at Night*
1983, oil on paper, 63 x 51 cm

*Gardiner Street 1*
1984, oil on canvas, 118 x 86 cm

*Gardiner Street*
1984, oil on canvas, 147 x 99 cm

*Italian Landscape*   1984, mixed media on paper, 35 x 25 cm, 24 x 30 cm

*Self Portrait, Italy*
1984, oil on paper, 71 x 97 cm

*Babuscas*
1987, oil on canvas, 36 x 31 cm

*Heike*
c.1987, oil on paper, 59 x 71 cm

*Temple Bar*
c.1988, oil on paper, 76 x 62 cm

*John Rogerson Quay, Evening*
1987, acrylic on paper, 61 x 74 cm

*The Ark, Eustace Street*
1990, oil on canvas, 94 x 103 cm

*Liffey Flags*
1987, oil on paper, 57 x 69 cm

*Camden Street*
1989, oil on paper, 66 x 89 cm

*Norseman, Eustace Street*
1989, oil on paper, 63 x 51 cm

*Self Portrait with Isabella Rossellini*
c.1989-90, oil on paper, 54 x 40 cm

40

opposite

*Annaghmakerrig 1*
1988, oil on paper, 50 x 74 cm

*Annaghmakerrig*
1989, oil on paper, 56 x 69 cm

*Loch, Annaghmakerrig*
1989, oil on paper, 57 x 70 cm

*Red House on Canal*
1990, acrylic on paper, 46 x 73 cm

*Annaghmakerrig, Path*
1989, oil on paper, 60 x 50 cm

*Boland's Mill, Grand Canal Basin*
1988, oil on canvas, 90 x 122 cm

*Sherkin Rocks*
1991, oil on canvas, 92 x 122 cm

45

*The Lee Bridge*
1991, oil on canvas, 91 x 62 cm

*South Gate Bridge and Beamish Brewery*
1991, oil on board, 83 x 107 cm

*Kent Street Station* II
1990, oil on canvas, 57 x 72 cm

*Kent Street Station* I
1990, oil on card, 60 x 69 cm

*Summerhill, Dublin Road*
1990, oil on board, 78 x 104 cm

*Cork Dockside*
1991, oil on board, 81 x 108 cm

pages 52-53

*Priestman 2*   1991, oil on canvas, 91 x 62 cm          *St Fin Barre's*   1991, oil on canvas, 139 x 92 cm

*Self Portrait Smoking*
1990, oil on canvas, 61 x 49 cm

# The Urban Scenario

JOHN MEANY

P at Moran's first studio was on the upper floor of a half-derelict building on Gardiner Street, just north of Dublin's River Liffey. The building was similar to many of those he painted over the following decade – dilapidated and cold, one of many Georgian houses waiting to be demolished. Yet its robust structure, and the traffic, people, weather and pollution outside, captivated him and became the source of his early sketches and paintings. Like many artists, he was attracted to the frenetic activity of a city centre, and his work reflects this colourful chaos. Either with line or brushstroke, his work exhibits a fascination with the movement of a city. Later, when he drew and painted landscapes, the same energy is evident, but I think that the urban scenario, with its crowded streets, bridges and cranes, produced his best work.

A group of us shared this formerly grand building, its dereliction admired for its previous beauty, and endured in an inhospitable state. Despite the freezing cold of winter, he always had a fire lighting, working continually on his early paintings of the streetscape of Dublin with tempestuous skies and rugged buildings. The studio offered him a bird's-eye view of the traffic, the people and the buildings which were crumbling around him. I remember him saying one day, 'I just paint what I see out the window.' That was an unusual statement at the time, when figurative painting, especially something as seemingly mundane as city views, were considered outmoded, even old-fashioned. Yet it was the immediacy of his surroundings, that he chose to observe, sketch and paint, which captivated and drove him. It was an approach which he continued to adhere to throughout the next decade, wherever he lived, and many similarities appear in his images of Cork ten years later.

His choice of subject and his disinterest in the largely conceptual abstract tenets of the day were part of a growing change in painting from around the beginning of the 1980s. While a student at Dun Laoghaire College of Art, he, and many others, were influenced by Brian Maguire and Patrick Graham. Both are now well-known and respected Irish artists, but twenty years ago their attitude and style went against the tide. Their agitated drawing, passionate brushwork and vivacious colour had a forceful impact on their students. In their different ways they projected an enthusiasm for a return to a direct, unfettered approach to drawing and painting. They were not isolated figures of course, and as the decade progressed New Expressionism became an international phenomenon. Rough drawing and painting became accepted modes again, painterly gestures and expressionistic marks were accepted, and representational images were no longer taboo.

Leaving college with his characteristic irreverence and disrespect for any artistic fashions, Pat worked on his vision of what he saw and wanted to express. As this retrospective shows, his concerns remained relatively unchanged over the following decade. Despite long trips to Mexico and Italy, which influenced him greatly, there is a perceptive unity in style throughout his career. The almost surreal undulations of water, the explosive clouds, the primitive looking cars and the sense of place remain consistent throughout. The drawings and sketches give us an insight into Pat's way of depicting his subject, whether urban landscape or portrait. There is an effort and exploration in his linear compositions, an attempt to capture an essence rather than render the purely pictorial. The paintings always have the skeletal drawing beneath, the daubs of colour suggesting the underlying search for a way to convince us of that reality. There is great energy and craft in his use of line, but in his paintings colour comes to the forefront. He shared his intense palette with the painters he admired – Soutine, Dufy, Jack B Yeats and Rivera. The greys and browns we associate with city streets are imbued with emotionally infused blues and reds, perfectly capturing the atmosphere.

Pat achieved a great deal in the decade before his tragic death. We can still wonder what he might have produced, but at least this exhibition and publication are here as a testament to his talent, and will bring his work to the wider audience he deserves.

Pat Moran's Studio
Gardiner Street, 1984

1
3

2
4

*Cork Dock Scene*
1990, pencil on paper, 42 x 60 cm

*Street Scene*
1990, pencil on paper, 29 x 42 cm

*Cork Dock Scene*
1990, pencil on paper, 25 x 36 cm

opposite

*Claire*
1981, pencil on paper,
38 x 26 cm

*Mo*
c1989, charcoal on paper,
64 x 45 cm (detail)

*Heike*
c1989, charcoal on paper,
60 x 42 cm

*Heike*
c1989, charcoal on paper,
60 x 42 cm

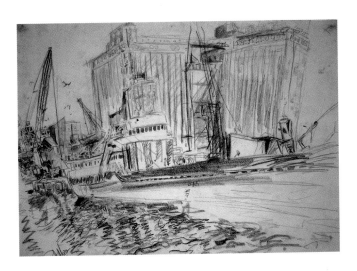

*Italian Landscape*   1984, pencil on paper, 21 x 30 cm

*Bernini Fountain, Rome*   1984, pencil on paper, 27 x 38 cm

# The Stubborn Romantic

GERRY KILBY

The tragic death of artist Pat Moran came as a great shock to all those who knew him. For Pat had a rare gift: apart from his talent as an artist, he had a charisma and depth of character that few possess but most aspire to. His easygoing casual charm, however, belied a deeper personality that was consistently striving to overcome his physical and environmental limitations in a battle to understand himself, his surroundings and the relationship between. Perhaps that could be said of many artists, but few possessed Pat's intellect and, above all, his stubborn romanticism. His art reflected this inner quest in the subject matter of his paintings. He painted things that he had a loyalty and an attachment to. He painted himself, his friends and his surroundings – a trend that could be seen even in his early work. Later the relationship with his subject matter was to become more intimate, but always there was a great sense of the love of life reflected in his work.

In 1984 he ventured to Italy to work as the caretaker of a house in a small town outside Rome. It was here in the peace and quiet of the Italian countryside that his art began to mature. He was fascinated by the brilliant sunsets, of which he did a number of studies. The techniques he learned here were to show through in his skyscapes of the much later work.

Cities, and in particular Dublin, seemed to hold the biggest challenge to Pat. The numerous studies and paintings he did in his studio in Gardiner Street and later in Eustace Street of cityscapes seemed to reflect a desire to understand the essence of the city, and, by doing so, find his place within it and his relationship to it. But it was in Cork city that he found a sense of place and purpose that had eluded him in Dublin. His work gained a new maturity and depth. One has only to look at one of his last and perhaps one of his best studies, that of St Fin Barre's Cathedral in Cork, to see the confidence and mastery of the artist. I remember in one of my many visits to Pat in Cork he took me to see the cathedral. As we stood below staring up at the cold grey Gothic edifice for some time, without talking, he turned to me and said, 'I'm going to paint that soon.' It was not so much a statement but more a challenge he was presenting himself, for Pat lived for the challenge. Some time later in his studio in Cork he showed me sketches he had done; in particular I remember there was one charcoal sketch which was magnificent. The cold, gothic cathedral had become a living organic structure, growing out of the ground like a great oak – old, wise and proud. The indifference was gone now, its huge steeples looked benignly upon the passerby. There was a lot of Pat in there.

GERRY KILBY is MD of Equinox e-Business Solutions. This piece was first published in *The Bar*, July-August 1993.

# Chronology

1961     Born in Portlaoise, Co Laois, on 7th November

1979-82     Attends Dun Laoghaire School of Art and Design. Completes foundation course and studies fine art for two years. Spends the summer of 1981 in Copenhagen working as a postman. Leaves college in 1982 and is commissioned to paint a mural for Ballinteer Health Centre.

1983     Resumes fine art studies at the National College of Art & Design, Dublin. Exhibits a large self-portrait in Claremorris Open Exhibition, Co Mayo. Moves into a studio in Lower Gardiner Street, where he continues to work, off and on, until 1986. It is here he first develops his interest in the urban landscape.

1984     Moves to Italy for a year, staying in Prima Porta, on the outskirts of Rome. Learns to speak Italian, cook and sketch outdoors in the warmth. Attends an etching course and exhibits in a group show at the Galleria Mafai, Rome.

1985     Leaves Italy in the early summer of 1985. Travels to Morocco and Spain before returning to Ireland and his studio in Gardiner Street.

*Pat was very congenial company. By turns erudite, coarse and very funny, not to mention being highly particular about the proper way to make an authentic Italian tomato sauce.*
                   – Hugh Lorigan on his time spent sharing a studio with Pat

Takes part in *Five Artists' Work* in Ballyfermot library. From August to December participates in and completes the Irish Museum Trust Arts administration course.

1986     Works as exhibition co-ordinator for the Liberties Association Thomas Street Heritage Project from January to June. Travels to Mexico to study mural painting. Becomes involved with the Artists Association of Ireland, a commitment he kept up throughout his life; he was on the board and later was to edit *Art Bulletin*. A large drawing of the view down Gardiner Street, *Grow with Irish Life*, is exhibited in the Independent Artists show at the Guinness Hopstore. Moves to Temple Bar, first to Temple Lane and later to 16 Eustace Street. His daughter, Banbha McCann, is born on 27th November.

1987     Takes part in a three-person show, *Studio 16*, at the Peacock Theatre, Dublin.

*The prospect of another penniless weekend in Dublin looms large. It is enough to drive me into the studio.*
                   – letter written to Hugh Lorigan

1988     Designs and executes murals with the Inchicore Murals Project. *Local Colour* – his first solo exhibition – takes place at Temple Bar Gallery, Dublin. First residency at Tyrone Guthrie Centre, Annaghmakerrig, Co Monaghan. Takes part in National Portrait Awards, Dublin.

1989     *I'm planning to go and hide up in Annaghmakerrig for a few months later in the year, but meanwhile I'm trying to re-establish my grip on the urban landscape.'*     – letter to Claire Carpenter, 7 July 1989

Visits Annaghmakerrig for the second time. Moves to Cork's Fota House where he helps to catalogue Richard Woods' collection of Irish landscape paintings, or 'Brown paintings', as Pat called them.

1990    Takes part in the *Living Landscape* exhibition at West Cork Arts Centre, Skibbereen; which travelled to Arts Council Gallery, Belfast; Galway Arts Centre; Irish Life Exhibition Centre, Dublin. Shows in the National Portrait Awards at Arnott's, Dublin. Becomes a member of Cork Artists' Collective, and moves into a studio space in the library buildings of St Fin Barre's Cathedral. From this location he produces a steady stream of work. The stability and support of the Collective has a positive effect on his work.

1991    Becomes a well known-figure in Cork, with a busy schedule – Irish classes with the musician John Spillane at the Lobby, sessions at the Gables, An Spailpín Fánach and An Áras Irish club on the Mardyke. Becomes a citizen of the Peoples Republic of 1 Melville Terrace, Military Hill, a house he shares with the poet Gerry Murphy and the sculptor Annette Hennessy. Has his second solo show at Triskel Arts Centre, Cork. Teaches in the education unit of Portlaoise Prison.

*His rare talent for motivating and engaging with all people served Pat, the inmates and the staff of the prison well during his time there. The lucid and reflective qualities in Pat's art informed everything that he did and helped to counter the dehumanising side of prison life ... Pat was held in great esteem at the prison.*      – Brian Maguire, artist and Head of Fine Art, NCAD

1992    Moves back to Dublin and Studio 16. Not long after, he went with a group of friends to Sherkin Island in Roaringwater Bay, west Cork, for the long weekend at the end of May. It was there that Pat tragically drowned. He was thirty years old.

After Pat's death, Tony Sheehan – with the assistance of Leo McCann, Triskel Arts Centre and the Artists Association of Ireland – raised funds to purchase the painting *St Fin Barre's Cathedral*, and donated it to the Crawford Municipal Art Gallery's permanent collection.

1993    *The Blue Bag*, a cassette tribute to Pat Moran, was produced by Ned McLoughlin in 1993.

*The idea for this cassette grew out of the emotion, music and craic that happened at the 'wake' in Pat's studio the night following the day he was buried ... The title* The Blue Bag *comes from a saying Pat used sometimes which he borrowed from* The Tailor and Ansty, *by Eric Cross: 'The world is only a blue bag knock a squeeze out of it when you can.'*      — Ned McLoughlin, 1993

2003    Retrospective exhibition at Crawford Municipal Art Gallery, Cork, and Dunamaise Arts Centre, Portlaoise.

Pat Moran, 1981